EYE TO EYE WITH DOGS

BASSET HOUNDS

Lynn M. Stone

Rourke
Publishing LLC
Vero Beach, Florida 32964

www.rourkepublishing.com

PHOTO CREDITS: All photos © Lynn M. Stone

Title page: *Bassets enjoy a little horseplay.*

Acknowledgments: For their help in the preparation of this book, the author thanks Susan Belott, Barbara Kohl, and Brian and Janice Pechtold.

Editor: Frank Sloan

Cover and page design by Nicola Stratford

Library of Congress Cataloging-in-Publication Data

Stone, Lynn M.
  Basset hounds / Lynn M. Stone.
    p. cm. -- (Eye to eye with dogs II)
  Includes bibliographical references and index.
  ISBN 1-59515-291-1 (hardcover)
  1. Basset hound--Juvenile literature. I. Title. II. Series: Stone, Lynn M. Eye to eye with dogs II.
  SF429.B2S763 2004
  636.753'6--dc22

                                                                    2004008022

Printed in the USA

CG/CG

Table of Contents

The Basset Hound   5

The Dog for You?   11

Bassets of the Past   17

Looks   20

A Note about Dogs   22

Glossary   23

Index   24

Further Reading/Website   24

This basset pup's expression seems to ask,
"Could things possibly be worse?"

The Basset Hound

Everyone knows the basset hound by its "sad" eyes and "poor-ole-me" expression. But don't be fooled by that expression. The basset hound is a tail-wagging and loving dog, ideal for many families.

Bassets haven't always been family dogs. The first basset hounds were used largely to **track** small game for hunters.

BASSET FACTS

Weight: 40-75 pounds
          (18-34 kilograms)
Height: 13-15 inches
          (33-38 centimeters)
Country of Origin:
          France
Life Span: 8-12 years

Beagle hounds share basset colors, but beagles are much smaller and quicker.

Bassets are natural hunters and great trackers because they have a keen sense of smell. Because they are short-legged, bassets live close to the ground. That puts a basset's nose close to the scent trail left by another animal.

With its forehead wrinkled and ears dragging, a basset hound eagerly follows a scent.

Basset hounds raised as show dogs are usually too short-legged to be hunters.

Bassets are one of the dog **breeds** known as **scenthounds**. Bloodhounds and beagles are also scenthounds. In fact, the bloodhound is probably the only dog with a sharper sense of smell than the basset.

The basset you meet today is not likely to be a trained hunter. A few basset owners, however, do still raise dogs for rabbit hunting.

Gentleness is a big part of the basset's nature.

*Always looking for human attention, tail-wagging bassets
surround their owners.*

These bassets tend to be lighter-
boned and longer-legged than stay-at-
home bassets. Bassets, like other
hounds, often hunt in packs.

Bassets have nothing against relaxing on a warm spring day.

The Dog for You?

People love the basset for its looks, its mild manner, and its **affectionate** nature. The basset is, indeed, a gentle animal.

The basset can be somewhat of a couch potato, but it needs exercise to remain healthy.

When exercising their dogs, basset owners are careful to keep their dogs on leash or in an enclosed yard. A free-roaming basset may begin to follow a scent trail and wander off until it is out of sight and lost.

Outdoors, the basset lives in a world of smells. A basset may become so interested in a scent that it tunes out its owner. That tends to make a basset "stubborn" in human terms.

The basset's short legs are misleading. Bassets are heavy dogs.

A basset hound, nose up, barks at a visitor.

People who want a "small" dog are often interested in bassets. But as anyone who has lifted a basset knows, they are *not* small dogs. They stand almost closer to the ground than a daffodil bloom. But a basset hound may weigh more than a Labrador retriever or a German shepherd.

Like other hounds, bassets are sometimes quick to bark and howl. That makes them good watchdogs.

*The basset's long ears and sad eyes are similar to
a bloodhound's.*

Like most dog breeds, the basset hound came to North America from Europe.

Bassets of the Past

In the early 1800s, the French wanted a keen-scented hunting dog that they could follow on foot. They **mated** a variety of short-legged hounds. One of the "new" breeds that resulted was the Basset Artesien Normand. This dog was similar to the modern basset.

Dog breeders later mated bassets with bloodhounds to increase the basset's size.

A bloodhound shares the basset's "sad" face and deep-set eyes, but not its short legs.

Basset pups are said to "grow into" their extra-long ears.

The first bassets reached the United States in the late 1800s. By the mid-1900s, the basset was a popular pet.

Looks

The basset's name came from the French word *bas*, which means "dwarf" or "low thing." The name is fitting because the basset hound has a full-length dog's body mounted on short, thick legs.

A basset's coat is short, its forehead is wrinkled, and its snout is long. Its ears are also long. The ears may drag the ground when the basset is sniffing the ground.

The basset's wrinkles—loose folds of skin—may trap scent.

This basset has typical hound colors: black, brown, and white.

When a basset trails an animal, the long ears may help stir up scent. And it's possible that the basset's wrinkled skin helps trap the scent.

Bassets may be the color of any hound. They are often a mix of black, tan, and white.

A Note about Dogs

Puppies are cute and cuddly, but only after serious thought should anybody buy one. Puppies grow up.

Choosing the right breed requires some homework. And remember that a dog will require more than love and patience. It will need healthy food, exercise, grooming, a warm, safe place in which to live, and medical care.

A dog can be your best friend, but you need to be its best friend, too.

For more information about buying and owning a dog, contact the American Kennel Club at http://www.akc.org/index.cfm or the Canadian Kennel Club at http://www.ckc.ca/.

Glossary

affectionate (uh FEC shun ut) — showing friendliness toward another creature

breeds (BREEDZ) — particular kinds of domestic animals within a larger, closely related group, such as the basset breed within the dog group

mated (MAYT ud) — to have been paired with another dog for the purpose of having pups

scenthounds (CENT HOWNDZ) — the hound breeds that hunt largely by using their sense of smell, rather than their sense of sight

track (TRACK) — to follow the trail or scent of an animal

Index

Basset Artesien
 Normand   17

bloodhound   18

breeds   7

coat   20

ears   20, 21

exercise   11

hounds   9, 14, 17

hunters   5, 6, 8

scent   12, 21

scenthounds   7

sense of smell   6

watchdogs   14

Further Reading

Carroll, David L. *The ASPCA Complete Guide to Pet Care.* Plume, 2001.
Fogle, Bruce. *The Dog Owner's Manual.* DK Publishing, 2003.
Puskas, Lisa. *Basset Hound.* TFH Publications, 2001.

Website to Visit

Basset Hound Club of America at www.basset-bhca.org

About the Author

Lynn M. Stone is the author of more than 400 children's books. He is a talented natural history photographer as well. Lynn, a former teacher, travels worldwide to photograph wildlife in its natural habitat.